P9-DNQ-430

WRECK THIS JOURNAL

TO CREATE IS TO DESTROY

BY KERI SMITH

PENGUIN BOOKS

PENGUIN BOOKS
AN IMPRINT OF PENGUIN RANDOM HOUSE LLC
375 HUDSON STREET
NEW YORK, NEW YORK 10014
PENGUIN.COM

FIRST PUBLISHED IN THE UNITED STATES OF AMERICA BY PERIGEE, AN IMPRINT OF PENGUIN GROUP (USA) INC., 2007
PERIGEE EXPANDED EDITION PUBLISHED IN 2012
PUBLISHED IN PENGUIN BOOKS 2016

COPYRIGHT © 2007, 2012 BY KERI SMITH
ART AND DESIGN BY KERI SMITH
PENGUIN SUPPORTS COPYRIGHT. COPYRIGHT FUELS CREATIVITY, ENCOURAGES DIVERSE VOICES, PROMOTES FREE SPEECH, AND CREATES A VIBRANT CULTURE. THANK YOU FOR BUYING AN AUTHORIZED EDITION OF THIS BOOK AND FOR COMPLYING WITH COPYRIGHT LAWS BY NOT REPRODUCING, SCANNING, OR DISTRIBUTING ANY PART OF IT IN ANY FORM WITHOUT PERMISSION. YOU ARE SUPPORTING WRITERS AND ALLOWING PENGUIN TO CONTINUE TO PUBLISH BOOKS FOR EVERY READER.

EXPANDED EDITION ISBN (BLACK): 978-0-399-16194-0
EXPANDED EDITION ISBN (DUCT TAPE): 978-0-399-16270-1
EXPANDED EDITION ISBN (PAPER BAG): 978-0-399-16271-8
EXPANDED EDITION ISBN (RED): 978-0-399-16272-5

THE LIBRARY OF CONGRESS HAS CATALOGED THE ORIGINAL EDITION AS FOLLOWS:

SMITH, KERI.
WRECK THIS JOURNAL : TO CREATE IS TO DESTROY / BY KERI SMITH.
P. CM
ISBN-13: 978-0-399-53346-4
1. SMITH, KERI. I. TITLE.
NC139.S5665A4 2007
153.35 DC22 2006050329

PRINTED IN THE UNITED STATES OF AMERICA
20 22 23 21

SOME OF THE ACTIVITIES SUGGESTED IN THIS BOOK MAY NOT BE APPROPRIATE FOR UNSUPERVISED CHILDREN.

WARNING: DURING THE PROCESS OF THIS BOOK YOU WILL GET DIRTY. YOU MAY FIND YOURSELF COVERED IN PAINT, OR ANY OTHER NUMBER OF FOREIGN SUBSTANCES. YOU WILL GET WET. YOU MAY BE ASKED TO DO THINGS YOU QUESTION. YOU MAY GRIEVE FOR THE PERFECT STATE THAT YOU FOUND THE BOOK IN. YOU MAY BEGIN TO SEE CREATIVE DESTRUCTION EVERYWHERE. YOU MAY BEGIN TO LIVE MORE RECKLESSLY.

Acknowledgments This book was made with the help of the following people: my husband, Jefferson Pitcher, who provides constant inspiration for living a full and daring life (some of his ideas ended up here). Thanks to the talented artists Steve Lambert and Cynthia Yardley-Lambert who helped me brainstorm ideas during a lecture on contemporary art. To my editor at Perigee, Meg Leder, who embraced and believed in this project from the beginning, your thoughts and sensitivity left me with so much gratitude. To my agent, Faith Hamlin, for continuing to believe in my artistic/creative vision. Thanks also to Corita Kent, John Cage, Ross Mendes, Brenda Ueland, Bruno Munari, and Charles and Ray Eames, whose ideas and perceptions continue to rip me wide open.

Dedicated to perfectionists all over the world.

THIS BOOK BELONGS TO:

WRITE YOUR NAME IN WHITE.

WRITE YOUR NAME ILLEGIBLY.

WRITE YOUR NAME IN TINY LETTERS.

WRITE YOUR NAME BACKWARD.

WRITE YOUR NAME VERY FAINTLY.

WRITE YOUR NAME USING LARGE LETTERS.

ADDRESS

PHONE NUMBER

* NOTE: IF FOUND, FLIP TO A PAGE RANDOMLY, FOLLOW THE INSTRUCTIONS, THEN RETURN.

INSTRUCTIONS

1. Carry this with you everywhere you go.
2. Follow the instructions on every page.
3. Order is not important.
4. Instructions are open to interpretation.
5. Experiment.
(work against your better judgment.)

materials

ideas
gum
glue
dirt
saliva
water
weather
garbage
plant life
pencil / pen
needle & thread
stamps
stickers
sticky things
sticks
spoons
comb
twist tie
ink
paint
grass
detergent
grease
tears
crayons
smells
hands
string
ball
unpredictability
spontaneity
photos
newspaper
white things
office supplies
wax
found items
stapler
food
tea / coffee
emotions
fears
shoes
matches
biology
scissors
tape
time
happenstance
gumption
sharp things

ADD YOUR OWN PAGE NUMBERS.

CRACK THE SPINE.

LEAVE THIS PAGE

BLANK

ON PURPOSE.

STAND HERE.

(WIPE YOUR FEET, JUMP UP AND DOWN.)

POUR, SPILL, drip,
SPIT, fling YOUR COFFEE
HERE.

POKE HOLES IN THIS PAGE USING A PENCIL.

DRAW FAT LINES AND THIN.

PUSHING REALLY HARD WITH THE PENCIL.

THIS PAGE IS FOR HANDPRINTS
OR FINGERPRINTS.
GET THEM DIRTY THEN PRESS DOWN.

COLOR THIS ENTIRE PAGE.

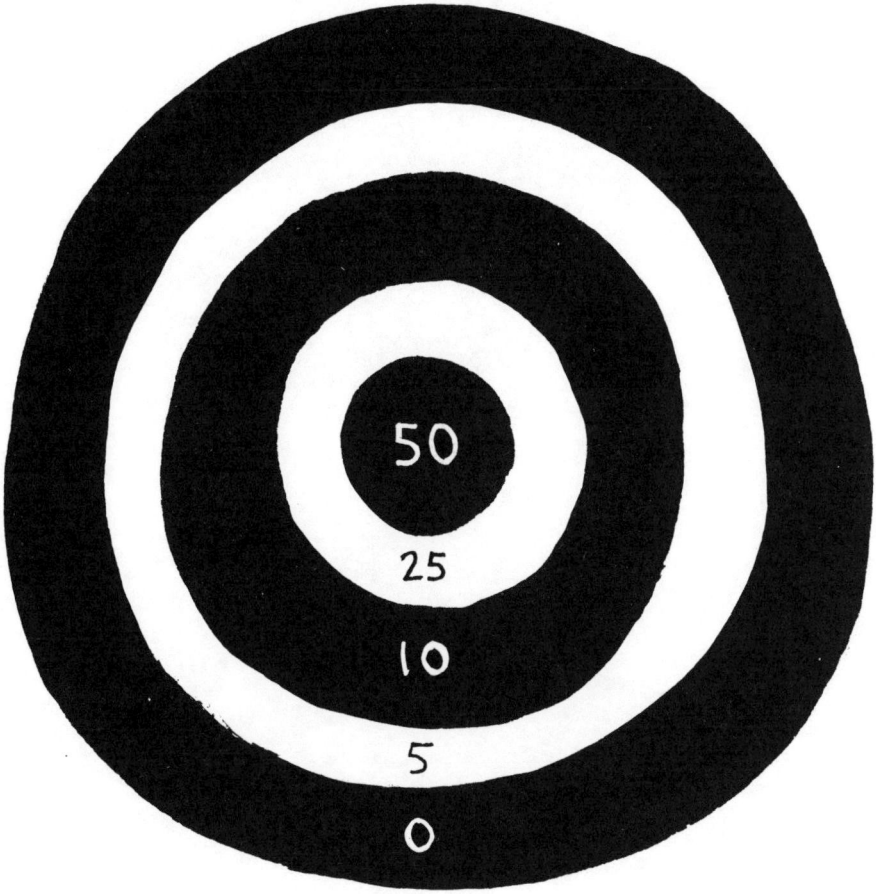

THROW SOMETHING

A PENCIL, A BALL DIPPED IN PAINT.

PRESS LEAVES AND OTHER FOUND THINGS

SCRATCH

USING A SHARP OBJECT.

DO SOME RUBBINGS WITH A PENCIL.

SCRIBBLE WILDLY,
VIOLENTLY, *with*
RECKLESS ABANDON.

TEAR STRIPS
RIP IT UP!

GLUE,
staple,
OR tape these
PAGES together.

draw lines

ON THE BUS, ON A

WHILE IN MOTION,
TRAIN, WHILE WALKING.

FILL THIS PAGE WITH CIRCLES.

Document your dinner.

RUB, SMEAR, SPLATTER YOUR FOOD.

USE THIS PAGE AS A NAPKIN.

CHEW ON *this.*

*WARNING: DO NOT SWALLOW.

MAKE A FUNNEL.

DRINK SOME WATER.

1. CUT OUT.

2. ROLL & TAPE.

3. ADD WATER & DRINK.

TEAR OUT

CRUMPLE.

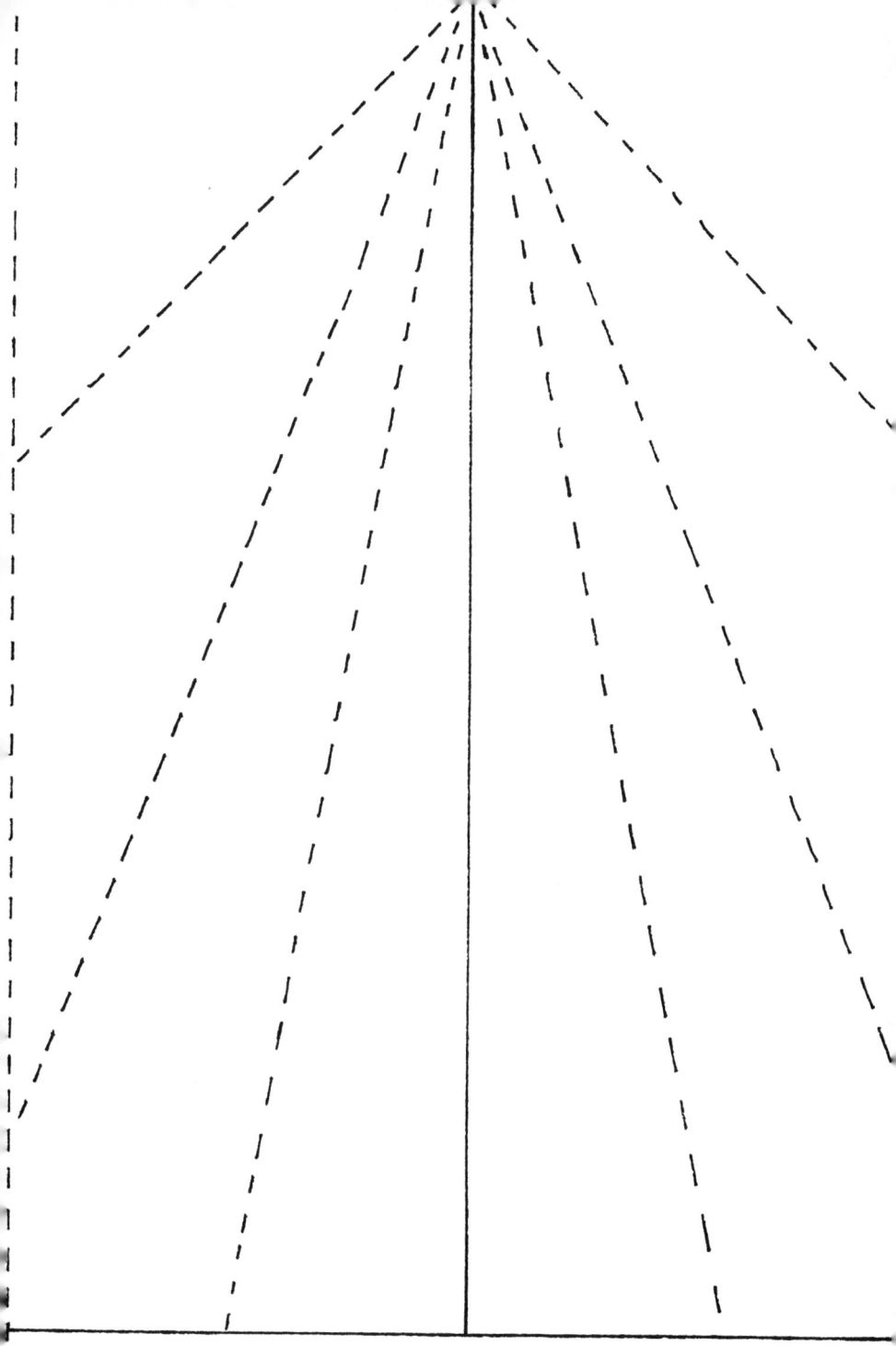

MAKE A PAPER AIRPLANE.

WRAP *something*

WITH THIS PAGE.

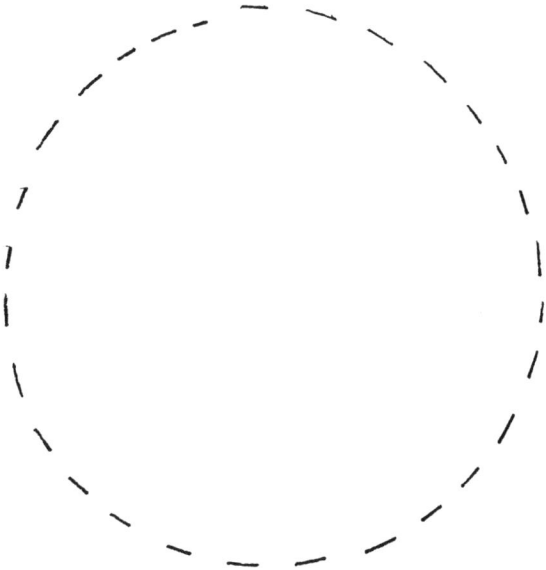

TONGUE PAINTING

1. EAT SOME COLORFUL CANDY.
2. LICK THIS PAGE.

WRITE ONE WORD

OVER AND OVER.

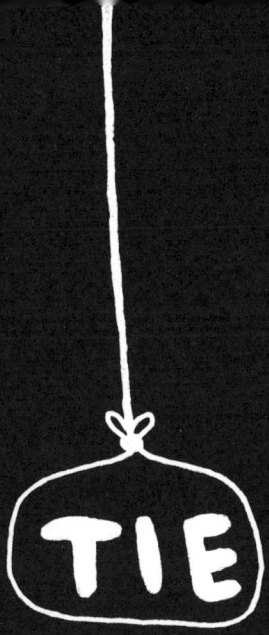

TIE A STRING TO THE *spine* OF THIS BOOK.

SWING WILDLY

LET IT HIT THE WALLS.

PICK UP THE JOURNAL WITHOUT USING YOUR HANDS.

CLIMB
UP HIGH
DROP THE
JOURNAL.

compost this page.

watch it deteriorate.

DO A *really* UGLY
(USE UGLY SUBJECT MATTER:
A BADLY DRAWN BIRD,

DRAWING

GUM, POO, DEAD THINGS, MOLD, BARF, CRUD.)

PLACE STICKY THINGS HERE.
(honey, GUM, syrup, glue, sucker, marshmallow)

PRETEND YOU
ARE DOODLING
ON THE BACK
OF AN ENVEL-
OPE WHILE
ON THE PHONE.

JOURNAL GOLF

1. TEAR OUT PAGE. CRUMPLE INTO A BALL.
2. PLACE JOURNAL INTO A TRIANGLE SHAPE.

3. HIT/KICK THE BALL THROUGH THE TRIANGLE.

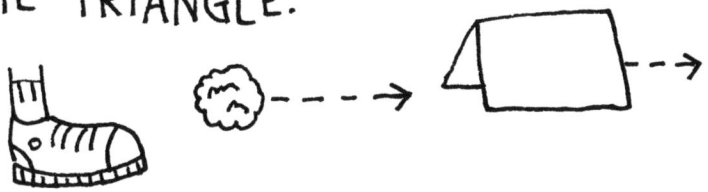

make a paper chain.

COLLECT FRUIT STICKERS* HERE.

*STICKERS YOU FIND ON BOUGHT FRUIT.

COVER THIS PAGE

USING ONLY office SUPPLIES.

BRING
THIS BOOK
IN THE
SHOWER
WITH YOU.

GO FOR A WALK, DRAG IT.

TIE A STRING TO THE JOURNAL.

RUB HERE WITH DIRT.

USE THIS AS A
test Page
FOR PENS, PAINTS,
MARKERS, OR ART SUPPLIES.

DRIP
SOMETHING
HERE.
(INK, PAINT, TEA)
CLOSE THE BOOK
TO MAKE A
PRINT.

Sew this
page

glue A RANDOM PAGE FROM A  NEWSPAPER HERE.

A PLACE FOR YOUR GROCERY LISTS.

COLLECT THE STAMPS OFF OF ALL YOUR MAIL.

TRACE THE THINGS IN YOUR BAG (OR POCKETS). LET THE LINES OVERLAP.

COVER THIS PAGE

WITH WHITE THINGS.

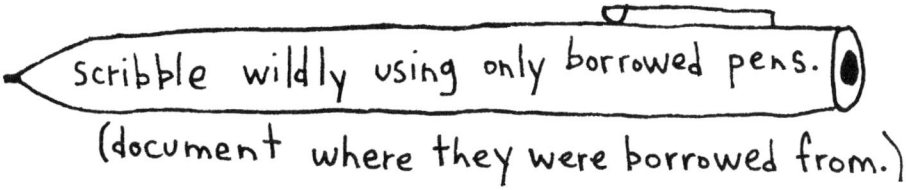
scribble wildly using only borrowed pens.
(document where they were borrowed from.)

MAKE A SUDDEN, DESTRUCTIVE, UNPREDICTABLE MOVEMENT WITH THE JOURNAL.

MAKE A MESS,
CLEAN IT UP.

DOODLE OVER TOP OF:

- ☐ THE COVER.
- ☐ THE TITLE PAGE.
- ☐ THE INSTRUCTIONS.
- ☐ THE COPYRIGHT PAGE.

FOLD DOWN THE CORNERS OF YOUR FAVORITE PAGES.

Page of good thoughts.

MAKE PRINTS USING AN INK PAD AND CUT VEGETABLES.

ASK A FRIEND TO DO SOMETHING DESTRUCTIVE TO THIS PAGE. DON'T LOOK.

WRITE
CARELESSLY.
NOW.

GLUE RANDOM
ITEMS HERE.
(i.e., things you find in your
couch, on the street,
etc.)

tear this page out.

PUT IT IN YOUR POCKET.
PUT IT THROUGH THE WASH.
STICK IT BACK IN.

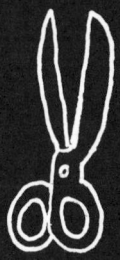

CUT THROUGH SEVERAL LAYERS

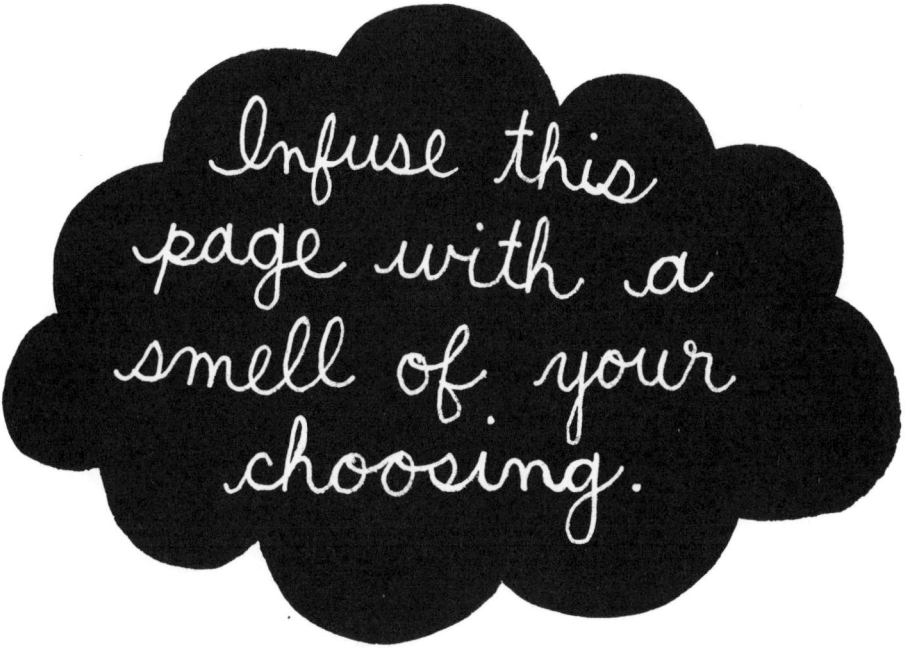
Infuse this
page with a
smell of your
choosing.

COLOR OUTSIDE
OF THE LINES.

CLOSE YOUR EYES.

CONNECT THE DOTS
FROM MEMORY.

HANG THE JOURNAL IN A PUBLIC PLACE.
INVITE PEOPLE TO DRAW HERE.

COLLECT YOUR

GLUE IT HERE.

POCKET LINT.

trace YOUR hand.

draw with
GLUE.

SAMPLE VARIOUS SUBSTANCES FOUND IN YOUR HOME.

DOCUMENT WHAT THEY ARE.
CREATE COLOR THEMES.

DOCUMENT A BORING

EVENT IN DETAIL.

CREATE A DRAWING USING A PIECE (OR SEVERAL PIECES) OF YOUR HAIR.

STICK PHOTO
HERE.

glue in a photo of
yourself you dislike.

DEFACE.

DRAW LINES USING
WRITING UTENSILS
(STICKS, SPOONS, TWIST TIES,

ABNORMAL
DIPPED IN INK OR PAINT.
COMB, ETC.)

fill in this
page when
you are really
ANGRY.

WRITE OR DRAW

WITH YOUR LEFT HAND.

FIND A WAY TO WEAR THE JOURNAL.

this page is a sign.
what do you want it to say?

START

CREATE A NONSTOP LINE.

SPACE FOR NEGATIVE COMMENTS.*

(* WHAT IS YOUR INNER CRITIC SAYING?)

DRAW LINES WITH YOUR PEN OR PENCIL.

LICK YOUR FINGER AND SMEAR THE LINES.

LOSE
THIS
PAGE.

(THROW IT OUT.)
ACCEPT THE LOSS.

A PAGE for FOUR-LETTER WORDS.

GLUE IN A PAGE FROM A MAGAZINE.

CIRCLE WORDS YOU LIKE.

write with the pen in your mouth.

GIVE
AWAY YOUR
FAVORITE
PAGE.

Write backward.

DOCUMENT
TIME
PASSING.

THIS SPACE IS DEDICATED

TO INTERNAL MONOLOGUE.

SCRUB THIS PAGE.

HIDE A SECRET MESSAGE SOMEWHERE IN THIS BOOK.

SLEEP WITH THE JOURNAL.

(Describe the experience here.)

WRITE/SCRIBBLE SOMETHING ON THE EDGES.
CLOSE THE JOURNAL.

WRITE A LIST OF MORE WAYS TO WRECK THIS JOURNAL.

1.

2.

3.

4.

5.

6.

7.

8.

9.

10.

11.

12.

STAIN LOG

DOODLE OVER TOP OF THIS PAGE ↓↓↓ AND IN THE MARGINS.

This is not an important piece of writing. The author of this work is writing with the intention of creating a body of text that has little or no meaning. It is merely a texture of sorts that the reader will view as a canvas. Hopefully it will simulate a book that is embedded in your memory, a book you had in your childhood, the one that you secretly wrote in with your crayons. Maybe you were scolded for this by someone.

It could be your first textbook, which you defaced with your pen, prompted by the previous owner's little scrawlings. It was not your fault. Textbooks are destined to be defaced, it is a part of their nature. You are not to be blamed. Anything as boring as a textbook deserves everything it gets.

Are you reading this? You are supposed to be defacing this page. Please stop reading at once! This is your chance to deface something.

Maybe it is not as alluring because you are being told to do it. In that case I command you to cease your drawing immediately! If you make one more mark on this page the author will personally ban you from reading any future books of hers, in perpetuity (or for as long as she continues to make books, which will probably be for a very long time).

There are many things that you could do in place of defacing this page that would be more beneficial. Some examples include going to the dentist, cleaning out your fridge, washing the windows, cleaning under your bed, reading the entire works of Proust, arranging your food alphabetically, conducting a scientific study of polymer synthesis and its effects on the world, arranging your envelopes according to size, counting how many sheets of paper you have in your possession, making sure that all of your socks have partners, documenting your pocket lint (oh, yes you already did that earlier in this book), calling your mother back, learning to speak a new language, recording yourself sleeping, moving your furniture around to simulate a bus station, experimenting with new methods of sitting that you've never tried before, jogging on the spot for an hour, pretending you are a secret agent, decorating the inside of your fridge, drawing a fake door on your wall with chalk, conversing with your animal neighbors, writing a speech for a future award, walking to the corner store as slowly as possible, writing a positive feedback letter to your mail delivery person, putting a secret note into a library book, practicing finger strengthening exercises, dressing up as your favorite author, smelling the inside of your nose, memorizing *The Elements of Style* by Strunk and White, sitting on your front porch with a sign that says "Honk if you love birds," documenting the plants in your life on paper, smelling this book, sleeping, pretending to be a famous astronaut.

FIGURE OUT A WAY TO ATTACH THESE TWO PAGES TOGETHER.

RUB THIS PAGE ON A DIRTY SURFACE.

COLLECT
THE LETTER
"W"
HERE.

COLLECT
DEAD
BUGS
HERE.

DRUM ON THIS
PAGE WITH PENCILS.

FLOAT
THIS PAGE.

FIGURE OUT
A WAY TO
FREEZE
THIS PAGE.

HIDE THIS PAGE IN YOUR NEIGHBOR'S YARD.

ROLL THE JOURNAL DOWN A LARGE HILL.

SELL
THIS
PAGE.

TURN
THE
BOOK
INTO
A
SHOE.

SLIDE THE JOURNAL
(THIS PAGE FACE-DOWN),
DOWN A LONG HALLWAY.

SMUSH
SOMETHING
COLORFUL
ONTO THIS
PAGE.

SQUIRT
LIQUID
HERE
(TRY USING YOUR MOUTH).